Original title:
From Darkness to Light

Copyright © 2024 Swan Charm
All rights reserved.

Author: Mirell Mesipuu
ISBN HARDBACK: 978-9916-89-649-5
ISBN PAPERBACK: 978-9916-89-650-1
ISBN EBOOK: 978-9916-89-651-8

## Mosaic of Luminosity

Colors blend in vibrant dream,
Fragments dance in softest gleam.
Each shard tells a tale untold,
In this canvas, bright and bold.

Light cascades like gentle rain,
Whispers echo, joy and pain.
Together they create the whole,
A masterpiece that stirs the soul.

In shadows cast, the hues may fade,
Yet in darkness, light is made.
All the pieces, rich and rare,
Reflect the love that lingers there.

Glimmers sparkle, passersby stare,
In this art, we share and care.
A mosaic built from love's embrace,
In unity, we find our place.

In every crack, in every line,
Lies the magic, pure divine.
In this world of light and shade,
A mosaic of hearts not afraid.

## Shadows that Sing

In the twilight, dark takes flight,
Softly whispering, the night.
Shadows dance beneath the moon,
Echoing a haunting tune.

Voices linger in the air,
Melodies woven with despair.
Yet in the silence, hope abounds,
In every heartbeat, beauty sounds.

Figures move, entwined with grace,
In the dark, they find their place.
Rhythms pulse like distant drums,
In the stillness, magic comes.

Where shadows fall, there lies a spark,
A gentle light to guide the dark.
In every note, a story spins,
For those who listen, shadows sing.

Awake the senses, feel the calls,
From shadowed corners, music falls.
In the embrace of night we find,
A symphony that binds mankind.

## Whispers of Awakening

The dawn breaks soft upon the land,
With whispers like a gentle hand.
Nature stirs, her voice so clear,
Awakening all that we hold dear.

Morning dew on petals lies,
Reflecting all the waking sighs.
Sunlight kisses every leaf,
In silence, we find our belief.

A tapestry of sounds arise,
Birds take flight and fill the skies.
Each moment, a breath anew,
In whispers, dreams begin to brew.

From slumber deep, the world begins,
Life unfolds and each heart spins.
In the embrace of morning's glow,
We find the strength to let love flow.

Awake, arise, let spirits soar,
Embrace the moments we adore.
In whispers soft, the day begins,
A dance of life where love wins.

## The Light Garden

In the garden where the sunlight plays,
Colors bloom in warm arrays.
Petals shimmer, leaves embrace,
Nature's smile upon our face.

The paths are lined with vibrant hues,
Every step a tale imbues.
Whispers carried on the breeze,
In this haven, hearts find ease.

Dancing shadows, soft and light,
Filling the air with pure delight.
In every corner, joy abounds,
In the garden, life surrounds.

Each flower holds a timeless grace,
In their blooms, we find our place.
Together, we rise, hand in hand,
In the warmth of this light land.

In twilight moments, stars will gleam,
Reflecting all that we could dream.
In the light garden, we shall play,
Embracing love at the end of day.

## **Lost in a Ray**

In shadows deep, where light may fade,
A whisper stirs, in silence made.
Through tangled paths, my heart does roam,
In search of warmth to guide me home.

A fleeting glow, a fleeting dream,
Beneath the stars, I hear the stream.
Each flicker hints of what could be,
A solace found, my spirit free.

With every step, the world feels near,
The distant laughter, the echo clear.
Amidst the fog, a truth takes flight,
I lose myself, yet find the light.

In rays that dance and softly play,
I trace the lines of yesterday.
As dawn breaks through the heavy night,
I'm lost within this gentle light.

## Spirits Alight

In twilight's glow, we gather near,
With whispered dreams, we shed our fear.
The night unfolds, with stars in sight,
Our hearts ignite, as spirits light.

Together we weave the tales of old,
Of love and loss, both brave and bold.
In rhythms soft, we find our flight,
In every beat, our souls alight.

As shadows dance, our laughter rings,
A symphony of unseen things.
With open arms, we hold the night,
In every spark, our spirits bright.

We share the warmth of fire's embrace,
In every face, a sacred space.
With every breath, our hopes unite,
In this embrace, our spirits light.

## Beyond the Silent Abyss

In depths unseen, where echoes dwell,
A haunting peace, a whispered spell.
Beyond the void, a truth exists,
In solitude, the heart persists.

The shadows cast, they weave a tale,
Of dreams once bold, now frail and pale.
Yet through the dark, a voice will hiss,
A yearning spark, beyond abyss.

With each new dawn, the depths unfold,
Revealing paths, both brave and bold.
In every sigh, a chance to kiss,
The light that breaks, beyond abyss.

Through trials faced, we rise anew,
With courage found, our spirits true.
Together strong, we find our bliss,
In hope's embrace, beyond abyss.

## Halo of Hope

In a world where shadows grow,
A halo shines to guide us slow.
With tender light upon our face,
We chase the dawn, we seek our place.

Each step we take, a path we pave,
With hearts aligned, we feel so brave.
In warm embrace, despair won't cope,
For we are bound by this halo of hope.

The dreams we hold, like stars above,
In every heart, a glow of love.
Together strong, we'll never mope,
With every breath, this halo of hope.

As whispers rise and fears decline,
We find the strength in every line.
United here, we softly grope,
For light resides in this halo of hope.

## Whispers of the Dawn

In the quiet morn, a sigh,
Colors blend in soft reply.
Birds awaken, sweet and clear,
Nature's song draws ever near.

Gentle breezes start to play,
Chasing shadows of the day.
Sunlight spills through branches thin,
Awakening where dreams begin.

Whispers float on golden light,
Filling hearts with pure delight.
Morning's kiss, a tender touch,
Promises of hope as such.

As the world begins to wake,
Every moment, joys we make.
Life unfolds with each new ray,
Whispers of the dawn's ballet.

In the canvas of the sky,
Colors dance, they ripple high.
Nature's hymn, serene, profound,
Echoing the joy we've found.

## A Journey Through Shadow

In shadows deep where secrets dwell,
Whispers rise, a longing swell.
Through the dark, we seek the light,
Navigating the starless night.

Every step on this unknown road,
Carries dreams, a heavy load.
Yet within the heart ignites,
A flame that flickers, fiercely bright.

Through valleys low and mountains tall,
We confront the darkest call.
A journey carved by fear and hope,
With every breath, we learn to cope.

Hand in hand, we brave the storm,
Finding strength in love's warm form.
Illusions fade, we start to see,
The path ahead holds destiny.

Emerging from the twilight's clutch,
Finding courage in the touch.
The dawn unfolds, shadows release,
A journey wrapped in sweet release.

## **Radiance Unveiled**

A flicker bright, a spark ignites,
Unveiling dreams on starry nights.
Within our souls, a fire burns,
Radiance calls, our hearts it turns.

With every challenge, light will flow,
Guiding us where we must go.
In the darkness, fear may creep,
Yet in our hearts, faith runs deep.

As the layers slowly peel,
Revealing truths that we can feel.
The strength within begins to rise,
Transforming doubts into the skies.

In every moment, golden chance,
To dance with life in bold romance.
Radiance blooms where shadows fell,
A story only time can tell.

Let the light within us shine,
Transforming all, the world divine.
With every heartbeat, we unveil,
Our radiance, a timeless trail.

## **The Awakening of Hope**

In the quiet dawn of day,
Hope arrives in soft array.
Filling hearts with warmth anew,
Wrapping dreams in skies so blue.

Gentle whispers in the breeze,
Carry tales that soothe and please.
Each moment brings a chance to mend,
The scattered pieces we can tend.

Waking dreams from slumber's grip,
As we sail on joy's sweet trip.
Through the shadows, we will glide,
Hand in hand, with love as guide.

Hope ignites in every heart,
A sacred bond, a work of art.
Shining bright, it lights the way,
Transforming night to golden day.

In the embrace of joy's sweet light,
Awakening the soul's pure sight.
For in the dawn, we come to know,
The beauty born from seeds of hope.

# Resplendent Transformation

In shadows deep, the whispers play,
A heart reborn in the light of day.
With every tear, a spark ignites,
The soul ascends to higher heights.

Fleeting dreams, once lost to time,
Awaken now, in rhythm and rhyme.
Colors blend, in hues so bright,
A tapestry spun from day to night.

Nature's brush, it paints the scene,
A dance of hope, a vibrant green.
From barren lands, new life will sprout,
In this embrace, we find our route.

In every trial, the lesson learned,
Through ashes rise, the fire burned.
Embrace the change, let fears release,
In transformation, we find our peace.

The journey shapes, the heart refines,
In every twist, the spirit shines.
Resplendent glow, from within it beams,
A life renewed, infused with dreams.

## The Dawn's Immortal Song

At twilight's edge, the silence sighs,
As stars fade slow from ancient skies.
A melody born of the night,
Awakens softly with the light.

The sun ascends, a golden hue,
Kissing the earth with warmth anew.
Each ray a note in harmony,
A symphony of destiny.

In every breath, a promise made,
Through darkened paths, unafraid.
The dawn's embrace, a cherished friend,
In its glow, our spirits mend.

With every morning, hope will soar,
A hymn of life, forevermore.
The beauty found in every dawn,
A reminder of the light we've drawn.

Resounding sweet, the song it weaves,
In hearts it stirs, as the world believes.
The dawn's immortal song will stride,
Guiding souls through every tide.

## Life After the Eclipse

In shadows cast where silence dwells,
A tale unfolds, as darkness tells.
With every phase, a lesson gained,
In life's embrace, we're unchained.

The moon obscures but clears the way,
For brighter skies that greet the day.
In fleeting moments, fear will fade,
A vibrant world, in sunlight laid.

Resilience blooms like flowers wild,
From barren earth, the spirit's child.
Each petal whispers of the light,
In afterglow, our hearts take flight.

Forgive the past, embrace the grace,
With every dawn, a new embrace.
Life's tapestry, stitched with care,
In every thread, love's colors flare.

So dance once more, beneath the sun,
In life after, we are one.
The eclipse fades, but we remain,
In hope's bright glow, we break the chain.

## When Night Meets Day

Whispers of dusk embrace the dawn,
Shadows dance as light is born.
Silent wishes ride the breeze,
Nature holds her breath with ease.

Stars retreat, their glow fades out,
Colors blend without a doubt.
Morning breaks with golden rays,
A new beginning softly plays.

Chasing dreams through hues of light,
Birds take flight, a glorious sight.
The world awakens, hope renewed,
In every heart, a spark pursued.

Night and day in sweet embrace,
A gentle touch, a holy grace.
In harmony, they intertwine,
Creating moments, pure, divine.

With every sunrise, we are free,
To find the magic, you and me.
When night meets day, let spirits soar,
Together, we will seek once more.

## Illuminated Paths

Footsteps lead through twinkling light,
Guiding us through the darkest night.
Each flicker shines with stories told,
Ancient whispers, brave and bold.

Winding roads beneath the stars,
Healing journeys, healing scars.
In every glow, a chance to see,
The beauty of what's meant to be.

Every corner, a new embrace,
Paths illuminated, time and space.
Together we roam, hand in hand,
Through vibrant dreams, in wonderland.

With every turn, the heart ignites,
A tapestry of hopes and sights.
Illuminated, we stand tall,
Finding courage through it all.

As shadows fade, the dawn anew,
Guides us onward in what we do.
With every step, a spark unfolds,
Illuminated paths and stories bold.

## The Rise of Bravery

In the depths where silence dwells,
A stirring pulse, a story swells.
Courage blooms in hidden grace,
A heart prepared to face its place.

Whispers rise, the doubts subside,
In every fear, a spark of pride.
With every challenge, strength does grow,
The rise of bravery, a steady glow.

Through storms and shadows, we advance,
In every trial, we take a chance.
Unity binds us, hand in hand,
Our spirits fierce, we make our stand.

From ashes, we shall soar and sing,
Together, forged through everything.
Resilience echoes in the air,
A testament to those who dare.

As dawn emerges, hearts take flight,
With newfound fire, we embrace the fight.
The rise of bravery, bold and clear,
In every heartbeat, it draws near.

# Flickers of Joy in Gloom

In shadows cast by heavy clouds,
A spark ignites beneath the shrouds.
Flickers dancing in the night,
Soft reminders, love's pure light.

Through battles fought and tears that fall,
We gather strength, we stand tall.
In every sigh, there's room for light,
Flickers of joy in darkest plight.

Hope whispers sweetly through the pain,
In every loss, there's much to gain.
Laughter echoes through the gloom,
Together, we shall brightly bloom.

Reach for kindness, let it shine,
In every heart, a love divine.
Flickers turn to blazing flames,
Breaking free from quiet chains.

United in this journey true,
We'll light the way for me and you.
In every moment, let love loom,
Flickers of joy in all the gloom.

## Colors of the Heart

In the canvas of the sky,
Vibrant red and serene blue,
Every shade whispers love,
A melody pure and true.

Golden rays touch the ground,
With every heartbeat they shine,
A palette of hopes unbound,
In the colors, we align.

Emerald greens in the trees,
Nature's breath, soft and sweet,
In each hue, a gentle peace,
Where life's rhythm finds its beat.

Indigo dreams softly stir,
Under the cloak of the night,
Every glance a subtle blur,
Colors dance in soft light.

Together in this bright art,
We sketch our stories each day,
Painting life with every part,
In colors that never fray.

## Serenity After the Storm

The storm fades with a gentle sigh,
Clouds retreat, the sun does gleam,
A fresh calm fills the sky,
Nature's sweet, soft dream.

Tears washed down the wild terrain,
Leave behind a vibrant glow,
In the stillness, peace remains,
Gentle whispers of the flow.

Raindrops glisten on the leaves,
Tiny jewels, a fleeting grace,
The heart learns, the spirit believes,
In this quiet, we find our place.

Birds sing praises, high and clear,
Songs of joy fill the air,
Emerging from the shadows here,
Life renewed, hearts laid bare.

Breathe in deep this fragrant earth,
Appreciate the calm we earn,
In storms, there's profound worth,
For in silence, we return.

## Songs of Daylight

Morning breaks with a soft glow,
Birds awaken with their cheer,
In the sunlight, dreams take flow,
A new day bright and clear.

Whispers of the wind, so light,
Caress the trees in gentle dance,
Nature's chorus takes its flight,
Inviting all to take a chance.

Every beam a note on high,
In the symphony of dawn,
Together we let worries fly,
As day unfolds, we carry on.

Golden rays paint the horizon,
Embrace the warmth on our skin,
Life's orchestra is rising,
In the moment, we begin.

Underneath the azure sky,
We find our rhythm and our song,
With every heartbeat, we comply,
In the daylight, we belong.

## Tracing the Path of Sunbeams

Sunbeams dance through branches bright,
A path of warmth across the ground,
Leading where the heart takes flight,
In their golden arms, we're found.

They flicker through the leaves above,
A gentle guide in the green,
Whispers of nature's endless love,
In this light, all is serene.

Follow the trail where shadows play,
In the embrace of sunlit dreams,
Every step a bright ballet,
Life illuminated as it seems.

Moments captured in a ray,
Fleeting joys in brilliant hues,
In their glow, worries drift away,
Leaving us with endless views.

In this dance of light so rare,
We learn to cherish what we find,
Tracing the path beyond compare,
Sunbeams weaving hearts entwined.

## **Chasing the First Light**

In the quiet dawn's embrace,
The shadows slowly fade away,
Whispers of a brand new day,
Awaken dreams that brightly play.

Golden beams through branches dance,
Painting skies with hues so bright,
Hope emerges, takes a stance,
Chasing after morning's light.

Birds take flight in joyous tunes,
Their melodies, a sweet delight,
Carrying the song of moons,
Into the heart of morning's bright.

With each step, we wander near,
The world unfolds, a vibrant sight,
Every moment draws us here,
Chasing after first light's bite.

## **When Glimmers Ignite**

In a world of dull gray skies,
A spark begins to come alive,
Flickers in the hopeful eyes,
A heart anew begins to thrive.

Stars above like dreams in flight,
Shimmering with a gentle grace,
When glimmers ignite, souls take height,
In darkness, beauty finds its place.

Courage blossoms, fears subside,
As shadows dance in soft retreat,
With every struggle, faith is tied,
To every heartbeat, love's heartbeat.

Hope ignites, a blaze we crave,
In unity, we find our way,
Together, strong and bold, we save,
A brighter dawn breaks with the day.

## The Horizon's Promise

As the sun dips low and sighs,
Colors bleed in soft embrace,
Beneath the stretch of endless skies,
The horizon holds a sacred space.

Promises whispered on the breeze,
Of journeys waiting just ahead,
With every step, the spirit frees,
Past echoes linger, softly shed.

The waves crash low against the shore,
Each ripple tells a tale untold,
With every heartbeat, we explore,
The mysteries of life unfolds.

Embracing change, we walk the line,
Of fading light and twilight's song,
The horizon's promise, bright and fine,
Guides us where our hearts belong.

## Conversion of the Soul

In stillness rests a restless heart,
Yearning for a deeper call,
A transformation, fresh start,
Awakens spirit, shatters walls.

Through trials faced, we find our way,
Lessons woven, threads of gold,
In shadows cast by night and day,
The soul's true beauty is revealed.

Chasing visions, dreams unfurl,
A dance of light through darkened haze,
The universe spins and twirls,
Guiding us through unseen ways.

With the dawn's embrace we rise,
Embracing flow, we learn to soar,
A conversion, wisdom in disguise,
Unlocking every heavy door.

# A Path Through the Gloom

In whispers soft, the shadows creep,
A winding trail where secrets keep,
Beneath the boughs, the silence hums,
A gentle song of night that comes.

With every step, the darkness sways,
A dance of doubt in the muted haze,
Yet hope flickers within the shade,
A guiding light that won't evade.

Through tangled roots and misty air,
A courage found, a soul laid bare,
In gloom's embrace, the heart will rise,
To greet the dawn, to claim the skies.

The moonlight weaves a silver thread,
Through tangled dreams that lingered, dead,
In shadows deep, the truth takes flight,
A path revealed to embrace the light.

## Illuminated Echoes

From hollow depths, a sound will dream,
An echo born from quiet screams,
In luminous bursts, the past unveils,
A tapestry of light that trails.

Each memory, a radiant spark,
Guiding the wanderers through the dark,
With every glance, the history glows,
The stories known, where wisdom flows.

In vibrant hues, the voices blend,
Resonating truths that never end,
A chorus sung in twilight's grip,
Where fleeting moments softly slip.

Illuminate what time has stored,
In every heartbeat, every chord,
Dancing with shadows that intertwine,
Revealing echoes, pure and divine.

## **The Serpent of Shadow**

In twilight's grasp, the serpent coils,
A creature born from silent toils,
With scales of night and eyes of fire,
A whispering muse, both dread and desire.

It weaves a path through dreams and fears,
Entwining fate with threads of tears,
A guardian fierce of the hidden realm,
Where shadows dance and darkness is helm.

Glimmers break the midnight's reign,
Revealing truths buried in pain,
Yet within its maw, a choice does lay,
To face the beast or drift away.

For shadows hold both light and dark,
In every bite, the soul's own spark,
Embrace the serpent, learn its song,
You'll find in shadows where you belong.

## Unmasking the Light

Beneath the veil of night's embrace,
A flicker stirs, a hidden grace,
Through layers thick, it yearns to shine,
To break the mold, to intertwine.

The masks we wear, the roles we play,
Conceal the truths we fear to lay,
Yet in the depths, a whisper calls,
To shed the skin, to break the walls.

Unmask the light that flickers bright,
In shadows deep, a heart ignites,
With courage found in fragile space,
To claim the truths that time cannot erase.

In every moment, a chance to rise,
To face the world with open eyes,
Unveil the spirit, let it soar,
In light unmasked, we are so much more.

**Nocturnal Secrets Revealed**

In the quiet of the night,
Whispers dance with the breeze,
Moonlight paints the shadows,
Secrets hang in tall trees.

Stars awaken one by one,
Their glimmer soft and shy,
While dreams weave in and out,
Underneath the velvet sky.

A nightingale's sweet song sings,
Calling to the dreaming souls,
With each note, the heart takes flight,
As the world around it rolls.

Rustling leaves share stories old,
Of lovers lost and found,
With every breeze that passes by,
In the night's hushed, sacred ground.

In the darkness, truth emerges,
Hidden gems of thought and lore,
Nocturnal secrets softly whisper,
Leaving hearts longing for more.

# When the Starlight Lifts

When the dawn begins to rise,
And the starlight starts to fade,
Colors burst upon the skies,
With a beauty gently laid.

Golden rays stretch far and wide,
Chasing night into the deep,
Hope and warmth in time collide,
Breaking through our restful sleep.

Softly, shadows fall behind,
While the sun ignites the day,
Nature calls with voice refined,
As dreams and worries drift away.

Morning whispers secrets sweet,
New beginnings in the air,
Every heartbeat feels the beat,
A promise waits for those who dare.

When the starlight lifts and glows,
Life awakens, fresh and bright,
Each moment, like a river flows,
Guiding us into the light.

## Glowing from Within

In the stillness of the night,
A spark begins to shine,
Deep within the heart of souls,
Where dreams and hopes entwine.

With every challenge we may face,
A light begins to grow,
Fueled by passion, love, and grace,
A brilliance we can show.

Each moment holds a chance to shine,
To let the inner glow break through,
Igniting flames that intertwine,
As we reveal what's truly true.

The warmth we share can light the dark,
And guide us on our way,
For glowing from within will spark,
A brighter, bolder day.

So trust the light that's deep inside,
Let it illuminate the night,
For in our hearts, we must abide,
Embracing love's eternal flight.

## The Bridge to Brilliance

Across the water, dreams take flight,
A bridge of thought, a path of light,
Connecting hearts in silent grace,
To share a world, a warm embrace.

Each step we take, a journey grand,
Where laughter echoes through the land,
With every bridge that we create,
We draw closer, not too late.

Together we can feel the spark,
Illuminating all the dark,
For every bridge we choose to build,
With unity, our minds are thrilled.

In kindness, let us pave our way,
Through every storm and sunny day,
For brilliance lies within our reach,
And love is what we truly teach.

The bridge to brilliance waits for us,
A path of hope, a road of trust,
Let's walk it hand in hand, my friend,
And cherish all that love can send.

## Rising Phoenix

From ashes cold, a spark ignites,
Wings unfold in the silent nights.
With pain endured, a strength is born,
The phoenix soars at the break of dawn.

In fiery hue, it paints the sky,
With whispered dreams, it learns to fly.
A tale of loss, yet love remains,
In every heart, its spirit gains.

Embrace the flames, let the past dissolve,
In fierce rebirth, all wounds resolve.
Through trials faced, it claims its right,
In every heart, a spark ignites.

## Awaken the Dawn

The night retreats, a whisper calls,
As golden light through silence falls.
With gentle hues, the world awakes,
In every heart, a promise breaks.

The flowers bloom, the songbirds sing,
A melody of hope they bring.
With every breath, a chance to start,
Awaken now, with open heart.

The sun ascends, the shadows flee,
In nature's dance, we're truly free.
Embrace the warmth, let worries cease,
Awaken the dawn, find inner peace.

**Hope in Every Ray**

Morning breaks, the world aglow,
In each soft beam, a promise flows.
Through clouds of doubt, a light breaks clear,
Hope in every ray draws near.

The golden sun, a beacon bright,
Guides our hearts through darkest night.
With every day, a chance to rise,
Hope shines forth, beneath the skies.

In shadows cast, we find our way,
The heart's resilience here to stay.
So gather strength, let courage play,
Hope in every ray leads the way.

## Journeying Beyond the Gloom

Through winding roads and heavy skies,
We seek the light where shadows lie.
Each step we take, though steep and long,
We carry forth a whispered song.

With hearts united, we walk as one,
In darkest times, we'll find the fun.
With eyes ahead, we face the storm,
In every challenge, a chance to transform.

Together we rise, together we dream,
In unity's strength, we'll gleam and beam.
So journey on, through dark and light,
Beyond the gloom, our spirits bright.

## Banish the Night

The stars fade away, one by one,
The dawn whispers softly, a new day begun.
Darkness retreats, with breath held tight,
Embrace the warmth, banish the night.

Shadows disperse with each gleam of sun,
Chasing the fear, allowing hope to run.
In this embrace, the soul takes flight,
Renewed in spirit, banish the night.

With colors ablaze, the horizon ignites,
Each ray a promise, as day invites.
Dreams awaken, soaring in light,
In unity we stand, banish the night.

The moon bows low, in graceful retreat,
With every heartbeat, the rhythm's sweet.
Let laughter rise, shining so bright,
Together we strive, banish the night.

## Threads of Light

In the fabric of dusk, whispers take flight,
Woven together, in strands of soft light.
Each moment a tapestry, vibrant and bright,
Highlighting dreams in the veil of the night.

With every heartbeat, a thread comes alive,
Connecting our stories, together we thrive.
With hope in our hands, we skillfully write,
The tale of tomorrow, in threads of light.

From shadows we rise, with the dawn's gentle kiss,
Embracing the warmth, we find our bliss.
Shared in our journeys, hearts burning bright,
In the tapestry's weave, we are threads of light.

Each strand a reminder of love's tender fight,
Joined together, a beautiful sight.
In harmony's dance, our spirits take flight,
Eternally bound, we are threads of light.

# Awakening from Obscurity

From silence we rise, with whispers of dawn,
Sunbeams like arrows, gently withdrawn.
With every breath, we begin to see,
A world reborn, a new melody.

Lost in the shadows, where dreams seem to fade,
Each moment a spark, in colors arrayed.
Awakening slowly, as fears dissolve,
In the tapestry of life, our hearts resolve.

With courage ignited, we step into day,
Casting aside what once led us astray.
Boundless horizons, no longer must we plea,
Embracing the light, awakening to be.

From deep within shadows, our voices resound,
With hope intertwined, our joy is profound.
In the warmth of the sun, we turn to decree,
Awakening bright, from obscurity.

## The Spirit of Daybreak

At first light's touch, the world starts to sigh,
Birds lift their voices, painting the sky.
The spirit of daybreak, fresh and anew,
Unfolds its embrace, a shimmering view.

With colors that dance on the edge of the night,
The sun breaks the horizon, a glorious sight.
Each heartbeat ignites, setting dreams in tune,
The spirit of daybreak, a jubilant boon.

Awake to a symphony, nature's sweet song,
With harmony whispered where we all belong.
In the warmth of this moment, our souls intertwine,
The spirit of daybreak, forever divine.

As shadows dissolve and the world comes alive,
We breathe in the promise of what we can strive.
In the dawn's gentle glow, let our spirits align,
The spirit of daybreak, a love so divine.

## **A Tapestry of Brilliance**

Woven threads in radiant hues,
Life's stories unfold, bright and true.
Each moment shines, a stroke of fate,
In this tapestry we create.

Colors swirl in a cosmic embrace,
Time intertwines, it leaves its trace.
Whispers of joy, shadows of pain,
Every pattern, a lesson gained.

Under the stars, a canvas grand,
Dreams come alive, as hearts expand.
With every stitch, a memory sewn,
In the fabric of life, we are never alone.

Infinite patterns beneath the skies,
Crafted with love, as the spirit flies.
In this tapestry, we find our role,
Each piece a reflection of the soul.

So let us weave with threads so bright,
Illuminating hope in the dark of night.
In this grand design, we forever aim,
Each thread a story, each life a flame.

# Lifting the Veil of Night

In the stillness, shadows creep,
Yet dawn whispers secrets to keep.
The moonlight fades, stars lose their glow,
As the world awakens, soft and slow.

Silent dreams begin to fade,
With the sun's rise, new paths are laid.
The veil of night is gently torn,
Embracing the light of a bright new morn.

Fresh petals bloom with morning dew,
All of nature sings, fresh and new.
Hope arises with every ray,
Lifting the veil, chasing night away.

In the light, truth finds its way,
Shadows retreat, come what may.
With every heartbeat, life takes flight,
In the embrace of a radiant light.

So let us cherish each day's new start,
For in each dawn, lies a beating heart.
With every sunrise, we grow and strive,
Lifting the veil, we come alive.

## Sunbeams Dance on Fractured Dreams

Amidst the ruins, hope remains,
Sunbeams glisten on shattered pains.
In every crack, new life will sprout,
From fractured dreams, we rise and shout.

Golden rays weave through the dark,
A symphony played by the lark.
In the quiet, beauty unfolds,
With each new dawn, courage beholds.

Time may break, but love will mend,
These shattered dreams we can defend.
For in the struggle, we find our means,
As sunbeams dance on fractured dreams.

Gather the pieces, rewrite the song,
Embrace the places where we belong.
With every sunset, let go of fears,
And trust in the journey of all our years.

So here we stand, brave and bold,
In the heart of the night, stories told.
Together we rise, as one we gleam,
Under the sunbeams, we reclaim our dreams.

# Rebirth of the Soul

In the depths of winter's chill,
Awakens life, a quiet thrill.
From ashes born, the spirit grows,
In stillness, the essence knows.

Seeds of change in fertile ground,
Miracles waiting to be found.
Breaking free from chains of the past,
With each breath, the shadow is cast.

Like a phoenix in the dawn's embrace,
The soul takes flight, a stronger space.
Transcending limits, reaching high,
With every heartbeat, we touch the sky.

Love is the fire that fuels the flame,
In the dance of life, we reclaim our name.
With hands wide open, we learn to receive,
In the rebirth journey, we dare to believe.

So rise from the ashes, embrace the light,
For every ending births a new sight.
In the cycle of life, we find our goal,
As we celebrate the rebirth of the soul.

## Illuminate the Journey

Stars whisper softly, guiding each step,
Through shadows and doubts, where dreams often wept.
The path ahead glimmers, with hope shining bright,
Each turn holds a promise, a new spark of light.

With courage we wander, hand in hand we walk,
Sharing our stories, in silence we talk.
The road may be winding, yet love lights the way,
In every encounter, we find what we say.

Through valleys of fear, we rise like the dawn,
With faith as our compass, we carry on strong.
Each sunset a lesson, each sunrise a chance,
To embrace every moment, and dance our own dance.

Every milestone welcomed, a chapter we share,
With laughter and kindness, together we care.
The journey may challenge, yet hearts intertwined,
In the fabric of friendship, true solace we find.

As we chase the horizon, both near and afar,
Our spirits together, we shine like a star.
With each step in rhythm, life's melody plays,
Illuminate the journey, in wondrous ways.

## The Canvas of New Beginnings

A palette of colors, we blend and we mix,
Each stroke tells a story, with shades and with tricks.
On canvas unwritten, our dreams take their flight,
Crafting our future, in boldness and light.

With every new sunrise, a fresh start awaits,
The echoes of morning invite us to create.
From whispers of dawn, to the chase of the day,
New beginnings unfold, in every array.

Through laughter and trials, we sketch our own tale,
Ink flowing freely, as we break every veil.
The past is a lesson, the present our stage,
In this vibrant tableau, we write every page.

Colors collide as the seasons all change,
Transforming our vision, in moments so strange.
With dreams intertwining, in symphonic play,
The canvas awaits, to design our own way.

Each brushstroke together, a journey so sweet,
In hues of connection, our lives intermeet.
Creating a masterpiece, bold and profound,
The canvas of new beginnings, where hope is unbound.

## Eclipsed Horizons

The sun dips below, painting skies in despair,
Shadows stretch far, as we breathe in the air.
Yet in the eclipse, some beauty we find,
A glimpse of the stars, by the darkness aligned.

As day slips to night, a veil softly falls,
Whispers of futures echo through walls.
The moon takes its throne, a silvery sign,
Illuminating paths where the lost souls entwine.

A stillness descends, as time whispers low,
In this fleeting moment, we let our hearts flow.
Though light may be hidden, it's never quite gone,
For hope still ignites with each break of dawn.

We search through the shadows, where secrets reside,
Some dreams feel eclipsed, yet they never quite hide.
With patience as virtue, we wait for the flare,
For horizons will shift, and the light will be fair.

Embrace the unknown, let the journey unfold,
For every eclipse brings a story retold.
In twilight we gather, with starlight in sight,
Eclipsed horizons, reveal the true light.

## Dawn's Whisper

In hush of the morn, when the world holds its breath,
A soft gleam of light dances, conquering death.
The whispers of dawn stir the soul from its sleep,
Inviting us gently into dreams we will keep.

As petals unfold, kissed by dew's tender touch,
The silence of night fades, as dreams mean so much.
With each amber ray, new beginnings arise,
Dawn's whisper ignites, painting hope in the skies.

In moments of stillness, we listen so close,
To nature's soft hymn, like a soothing prose.
The promise of daylight, a sweet, warm embrace,
In dawn's gentle touch, we find our own place.

With courage unwound, we step forth with grace,
The shadows behind us, we move at our pace.
Each heartbeat a rhythm, each breath a new chance,
Guided by whispers, we join in the dance.

As sunflowers stretch towards the radiant light,
With fervent resolve, we welcome the fight.
In the magic of dawn, where our spirits run free,
Whispers of hope, the world's symphony.

**Fading Footsteps in Twilight**

The sun dips low, shadows creep,
Whispers of night, secrets to keep.
Footsteps linger, fading away,
In the embrace of end of day.

Softly they echo, lost in dreams,
Murmurs of dusk, gentle seams.
Stars awaken, blinking bright,
Guiding the heart through the night.

Ghosts of laughter in the air,
Memories drift, a fleeting stare.
Time relentless, never still,
Yet in the silence, night does thrill.

The path behind grows dim and thin,
Veiled in twilight, where hopes begin.
Each step taken into the night,
A journey hidden from the light.

In the twilight's tender glow,
Fading footsteps softly show.
A promise whispered on the breeze,
That dawn will come, hearts at ease.

## Luminescence Rising

In the cradle of night, stars awake,
Whispers of light, the darkness they break.
Dewdrops shimmer on the grass,
Quiet moments, time must pass.

Colors dance in celestial streams,
Painting the sky with shimmering dreams.
Each hue a story waiting to tell,
Magic spun within the swell.

From shadows deep, a glow ignites,
Filling the world with radiant sights.
Hearts will lift as colors blend,
In luminescence, there's no end.

Hope ascends with each dawn's light,
Chasing the remnants of the night.
In the horizon, a promise glows,
The universe with beauty bestows.

So let your spirit soar and rise,
In the embrace of painted skies.
For with each sunbeam, dreams take flight,
And all is well in the morning light.

## Shards of Celestial Light

Across the heavens, a breaking dawn,
Shards of light, a new day drawn.
Each glimmer weaves a tale of grace,
In the vastness, a sacred place.

Softly they fall like feathers light,
Encasing the world in pure delight.
Hope ignites within the soul,
As stars align to make us whole.

Fragments of dreams in the sky,
Guiding the lost, they gently fly.
In their glow, we find our way,
As night surrenders to the day.

Let your heart embrace the glow,
In shattered beams where wonders grow.
For even in darkness, light persists,
Finding its way in glowing twists.

So stand beneath this cosmic sweep,
Let the light in, let your soul leap.
For every shard, a promise bright,
In the universe's eternal flight.

## Reclaiming the Dawn

Awake from shadows, break the bind,
A new day calls to heart and mind.
The night retreats, its grip now torn,
In the embrace of promise, we're reborn.

Sunrise whispers, hope renews,
Golden rays chase away the blues.
With each heartbeat, courage grows,
As light unfolds, the spirit glows.

Clouds may gather, storms may roar,
But within us lies a firming core.
Together we rise, hand in hand,
Reclaiming the dawn, united we stand.

The horizon stretches, dreams ignite,
In the morning glow, futures invite.
With every step, we make our claim,
In the dance of dawn, we find our name.

So breathe in deep, embrace the day,
For the dawn is ours, come what may.
In the light of morning, we shall see,
The power of hope setting us free.

## The First Glimmer

In the quiet dawn's embrace,
A light begins to break,
Whispers of the waking day,
Promises the shadows shake.

Softly glows the rising sun,
Painting skies with gold,
Every hue a story told,
In the morning, dreams unfold.

Birds will sing their crystal tunes,
Echoes through the trees,
Nature wakes from slumber's grasp,
Dancing with the breeze.

Moments melt like morning dew,
Glimmers of hope bloom,
In the heart, a fleeting spark,
Chasing away the gloom.

As day unfolds, we find our way,
In the light of truth,
Guided by that first sweet glimmer,
Of joy reclaimed in youth.

## Awakening to New Horizons

Beneath the expanse of azure skies,
Dreams begin to take flight,
Yearning hearts and hopeful eyes,
Chase horizons bathed in light.

Mountains rise above the vale,
With paths yet unexplored,
Each step forward, a hearty sail,
Toward the future we're restored.

Seas of change sweep gently near,
Waves of promise cresting high,
In every challenge, shed the fear,
To touch the vast and open sky.

Whispers of the winds advise,
Listen close and be aware,
In the stillness, wisdom lies,
Unlocking dreams that we all share.

With each sunrise, a canvas bare,
Awaiting strokes of our design,
Awakening to what we dare,
Embracing paths we choose to shine.

## Silence Before the Bloom

In the garden, hushed and still,
Awaiting life to come alive,
Between the shadows, whispers thrill,
As dreams beneath the surface strive.

Petals close, their secrets kept,
Yet promise hangs in the air,
With every sigh, the earth has wept,
For beauty hides beneath the care.

Mirrors of the night reflect,
Stars in silent reverie,
In this pause, we recollect,
The hopes that wait to be set free.

Nature holds her breath in grace,
In anticipation's glow,
Soon will come the vibrant face,
Of life that yearns to grow.

When the moment breaks at last,
Colors burst in wild embrace,
The silence winds up in the past,
And blooms in radiant place.

## Transcending Twilight

In twilight's grasp, the shadows play,
As day gives way to night,
Colors blend in soft array,
Bidding time to go light.

Stars emerge in distant dance,
Diamonds set in velvet deep,
In the coolness, dreams entrance,
And the world begins to sleep.

Moments linger, softly traced,
Silence spreads its gentle wings,
In the calm, our fears embraced,
Whispers turn to ancient songs.

Transcending borders of the day,
We find peace in twilight's charm,
Here, the heart can simply sway,
Wrapped in night's encircling arms.

As stars awaken, we release,
The burdens held too long in flight,
In this space, we find our peace,
Transcending the embrace of night.

## Colors of Renewal

New buds bloom with dawn's first light,
Painting the world in colors bright.
Whispers of spring in the gentle breeze,
Life awakens from winter's freeze.

Fields of green with flowers spread,
Painting the earth in hues widespread.
Joy dances in every vibrant hue,
A season reborn, so fresh and new.

Beneath the sky so vast and clear,
The song of nature, sweet and near.
In every shade, a story tells,
Of hope that blooms where silence dwells.

Gentle rains and the sun's warm glow,
Nurture the life that begins to grow.
From soil rich, to mountains high,
The colors of renewal catch the eye.

In every corner, beauty found,
In every heartbeat, nature's sound.
Colors of life in harmony,
A vibrant world, so wild and free.

## The Light Within

In the silence, a spark ignites,
A whisper of hope, the heart's delights.
Like a candle flickering in the night,
Illuminating dreams, guiding the flight.

Deep within where shadows play,
A glowing ember lights the way.
Through storms of doubt and winds that wail,
The light persists, it will not pale.

Every soul carries a flame,
Unique and fierce, yet never the same.
In moments of darkness, let it shine,
For in the heart, true magic aligns.

Through trials faced and battles fought,
The light within is never caught.
With every tear, it softly glows,
Strengthened by life, it ever grows.

In melodies sweet, it dances bright,
Guiding each step, pure and light.
Trust in the glow that you possess,
For within you lies a boundless grace.

## **Glowing Beneath the Surface**

Hidden treasures in depths unknown,
Radiate warmth, a quiet tone.
Beneath the stillness of the sea,
Life pulses softly, wild and free.

Coral gardens, vibrant and bright,
Glow gently in the fading light.
A world of wonder, a silent song,
Where mysteries dwell and dreams belong.

The currents weave with grace anew,
Dancing with secrets, ancient and true.
In shadows cast, bright colors gleam,
Whispers of life in a flowing dream.

Each creature swims with grace and ease,
In this realm where hearts find peace.
They shine in colors, bold and rare,
A language of love beyond compare.

Below the waves, in tranquil streams,
Every flicker ignites the dreams.
With every heartbeat, they exist,
In the depths where fear can't resist.

## In the Heart of Night's Embrace

In the stillness where shadows creep,
The night whispers secrets, soft and deep.
Stars twinkle like diamonds in the sky,
Watching over dreams as they gently fly.

Moonlight spills on the quiet ground,
In its glow, a magic found.
Crickets sing their lullabies clear,
While the world slows down, now free from fear.

Wrapped in darkness, comfort we seek,
A sanctuary where spirits speak.
Breath of the night, tender and mild,
Embracing the essence of each hidden child.

The soft rustle of leaves in song,
Reminds us here is where we belong.
In the heart of night, dreams take flight,
Illuminating hope with each silver light.

As dawn approaches, whispers grow faint,
Yet the night remembers, a patient saint.
In every heartbeat, a promise stays,
In the heart of night, our spirit sways.

**Unveiling Hidden Wonders**

In the garden where shadows dance,
Petals whisper tales of chance.
Beneath the leaves, secrets grow,
In twilight's glow, they softly show.

With every step, the earth will breathe,
Stories spun from nature's weave.
Hidden paths, we wander low,
Where magic stirs and rivers flow.

Gentle breezes carry dreams,
In silver light, the world just beams.
Every moment, treasures spark,
In silence deep, we leave our mark.

Through emerald fields, our spirits glide,
Unveiling wonders, side by side.
Each glance reveals a brand new hue,
Mirrored in the morning dew.

With every heartbeat, realms unfold,
A canvas rich with colors bold.
Together we chase the secrets spun,
In the heart of all, we are as one.

## Steps Toward the Sun

On the path where shadows fade,
We rise, the promises we've made.
Each footfall a song of light,
In morning's glow, we find our flight.

With the dawn, new dreams ignite,
Through struggles, we embrace the fight.
Every heartbeat, every run,
We gather strength, steps toward the sun.

Bright horizons call our name,
In this journey, none the same.
With open hearts, we seek the bright,
Guided by the stars tonight.

With every challenge, we will grow,
Facing winds that fiercely blow.
In the warmth of every run,
Together we rise, steps toward the sun.

So let the sky be our embrace,
As we weave in time and space.
With laughter, joy, and love's sweet fun,
Our journey leads us, steps toward the sun.

## Chasing the Horizon

Beneath the arch of painted skies,
We chase the dawn, where freedom flies.
With every stride, the world unfurls,
As dreams emerge in golden swirls.

Through rolling hills, we find our way,
With hearts that dance, we greet the day.
In endless fields, our spirits run,
Together strong, we chase the sun.

The horizon whispers tales untold,
Of daring souls both young and old.
We seek the beauty found in grace,
In every shadow we embrace.

Across the seas, where wild winds blow,
In twilight's haze, our passions grow.
With stars as guides, we journey on,
Chasing dreams until they're dawn.

For every step ignites the flame,
As we chase horizons, wild and tame.
In every heartbeat, we are one,
Together we rise, chasing the sun.

## The Lightkeepers' Tale

In a lighthouse by stormy seas,
Guardians stand with hearts at ease.
They guide the ships through dark and dread,
With beams of hope ahead, they tread.

Every night, the lantern glows,
Whispers carried by salty flows.
Tales of sailors lost and found,
In every echo, life resounds.

Through tempest's roar and gentle sighs,
They watch the dance of stars arise.
With steadfast hands and watchful eyes,
Each lightkeeper holds the skies.

A symphony of waves and stars,
Healing hearts and mending scars.
Together they weave tales of grace,
In the darkness, they find their place.

For every night brings stories grand,
Of journeys bold across the land.
In light they find their humble merit,
The lightkeepers hold the spirit.

## **Threads of Starlight**

In the velvet night, they weave,
Whispers of dreams that softly leave.
Each spark a story, bright and bold,
Tales of wanderers, yet untold.

Swirling 'round the cosmic sphere,
Threads of starlight, shining clear.
A dance of hope, a glimmer's flight,
Connecting hearts through endless night.

In the silence, truths unwind,
Glimmers of fate, all intertwined.
The universe hums a timeless tune,
Under the watchful gaze of the moon.

A tapestry spun with care,
Woven paths where souls can share.
Through the darkness, beauty flows,
The light of love forever grows.

So when you gaze at skies so wide,
Remember the stars, they abide.
In every twinkle, there's a thread,
Binding us close, though far we tread.

## Breaking the Chains of Dusk

As shadows stretch and daylight fades,
A whisper calls through twilight glades.
Hope is stirring, like the breeze,
Ready to break the dark with ease.

Chains of sorrow, worn and cold,
Shatter softly, strong and bold.
Freedom beckons with a sigh,
Beneath the canvas of the sky.

In the heart of dusk, we stand,
Reaching out, hand in hand.
With every heartbeat, chains will break,
Rising from all that's left in wake.

Stars ignite in the horizon's hue,
A tapestry of dark and blue.
With courage born from dreams once lost,
We'll conquer fears, whatever the cost.

Together we'll forge a path anew,
Through shadows deep, with spirits true.
Breaking the chains, we'll light the way,
For dawn is coming, bright as day.

**The Symphony of Morning Songs**

Awakening soft, the world unfolds,
Whispers of dawn begin to mold.
The sky is painted in golden light,
A symphony that banishes night.

Birds take flight, their melodies rise,
Notes of joy that kiss the skies.
Each sound, a brushstroke in the air,
Crafting beauty beyond compare.

Dewdrops sparkle on the grass,
Nature's gems that shimmer and pass.
In harmony, the world's aglow,
Creating rhythms that ebb and flow.

Sunbeams dance through leafy trees,
Swirling softly on the breeze.
The morning hums a lively tune,
Filling hearts, making spirits swoon.

In this moment, all is clear,
A symphony that draws us near.
With every note, the day begins,
In this sweet song, true life begins.

## Eclipsing Yesterday

In shadows cast from days gone by,
Memories linger, soft as sighs.
Yet in the distance, light is near,
Promising dawn and moments clear.

Yesterday's ghosts may linger still,
But forward we strive with iron will.
The past, a page, we turn and flee,
Into a future we long to see.

Cloaked in dusk, we shed our pain,
Embracing change, like a warm rain.
Each step we take, the weight grows light,
Eclipsing the darkness with our sight.

Hope unfurls like wings in flight,
Guiding us toward the bright.
No longer bound by what has been,
The sun will rise, and we'll begin.

So let the shadows fade away,
For in our hearts, we find the way.
Eclipsing yesterday, we shall stand,
Hand in hand, our dreams so grand.

## From Ashes to Aurora

In darkness fell the fiery night,
Yet embers dance with hopeful light.
Each breath a whisper, soft and low,
From ashes rise the seeds we sow.

The dawn breaks forth, a canvas wide,
With colors bright where dreams abide.
A journey wrapped in hues of grace,
From shadows' hold to love's embrace.

Through trials faced, the heart will soar,
A phoenix born to rise once more.
In every tear, a strength reborn,
From ashes, see the new day's dawn.

The stars align, a guiding hand,
In vast expanse of shifting sand.
With hope as compass, hearts awake,
Each moment lived, no path we fake.

In twilight's glow, we stand as one,
Embracing life, our battle won.
From ashes to aurora bright,
We forge our way, we chase the light.

## The Promise of Tomorrow

In the hush before the dawn,
Lies a promise we lean upon.
A whisper carried by the breeze,
Hope blooms gently among the trees.

With every star that lights the night,
A dream unfurls, a pure delight.
The future's canvas waits in grace,
With every heart, a sacred space.

From shadows cast, we find our theme,
The power held within each dream.
As whispers turn to songs of peace,
Tomorrow's dawn brings sweet release.

In every challenge, seeds are sown,
With courage fanned, we stand alone.
Yet hand in hand, we'll walk the line,
The promise made to seek the shine.

The path ahead may twist and bend,
But hope renews what hearts defend.
With every step, a tale we weave,
In tomorrow's light, we will believe.

## Shattering the Silence

In stillness deep, the echoes stir,
A voice within begins to purr.
Beneath the calm, a storm will rise,
Shattering the silence with cries.

In shadows thick, the truth will find,
The light that has been left behind.
With every heartbeat, courage grows,
A tale of strength that boldly shows.

The silence whispers tales untold,
Of dreams once bold, now shunned and cold.
Yet like the dawn, we break the chain,
With open hearts that dance in pain.

Resistance melts as voices blend,
In symphony, we will transcend.
Let echoes of our souls unite,
Shattering silence, winning the fight.

The battle's won, and yet we stand,
With open hearts, we take command.
For in our voices lies the key,
To shatter silence, set us free.

## An Odyssey of Illuminated Dreams

In realms where visions softly play,
We wander through the night and day.
Each step we take, a story told,
An odyssey where hearts unfold.

The moonlight dances on the seas,
Whispers of love ride on the breeze.
With every star, a wish takes flight,
Illuminated by gentle light.

Through valleys deep and mountains high,
We chase the dreams that light the sky.
With every heartbeat, magic grows,
A journey vast where wonder flows.

In colors bright, our spirits soar,
Chasing the dreams we can't ignore.
With every dawn, a chance to see,
An odyssey of what could be.

Together we weave tales of grace,
In timeless moments we embrace.
Illuminated, we rise and beam,
In this grand dance, we find our dream.

## **Shadows Break at Sunrise**

Shadows stretch across the ground,
A gentle whisper, silent sound.
The sun begins its rise anew,
Painting skies with golden hue.

Birds take flight in morning's light,
Wings unfolding, pure delight.
Nature stirs, the world awakes,
In every heart, a joy that breaks.

Colors blend, a soft embrace,
Hope awakens, finds its place.
With dawn's touch, the darkness fades,
As life begins, the peace cascades.

Mountains glow, the waters gleam,
Visions born from night's deep dream.
As shadows flee, the day ignites,
In every dawn, new futures bright.

Moments captured, fleeting, brief,
In sunrise, we find relief.
Embrace the day, let spirits fly,
For in this light, our dreams comply.

# **Echoes of Glistening Horizons**

Beyond the hills, where skies unite,
The echoes call, a siren's flight.
Waves of light dance on the sea,
Reflecting dreams, setting them free.

Beneath the stars, stories unfold,
Whispers of fortunes yet untold.
Through time's gate, our visions roam,
In the glimmer, we find our home.

Mountains stand with wisdom grand,
Guardians of this timeless land.
Every shadow tells a tale,
In glistening moments, we exhale.

Horizons stretch beyond our sight,
Embracing hope in fading light.
With every dawn, the past rewinds,
In echoes of what time unwinds.

Glistening paths await our stride,
With dreams alight, we shall abide.
Together we chase every gleam,
For in each heart ignites a dream.

## Embracing the Golden Hour

As daylight wanes, a soft embrace,
The golden hour reveals its grace.
Kisses of sun on weary ground,
In every glow, a magic found.

Time slows down, the world stands still,
Moments ripe, a sweet thrill.
Colors swirl in evening's breath,
With warmth that dances close to death.

Fireflies twinkle, a guiding light,
In this hour, all feels right.
Gentle whispers of the breeze,
Embrace our hearts, put us at ease.

The horizon blushes, a sacred hue,
As day bids night a fond adieu.
In twilight's glow, we find our peace,
Life's simple joys, they never cease.

Embracing moments, fleeting, rare,
In the golden hour, souls laid bare.
Together lingering, side by side,
In this magic, we confide.

## **Slumbering Stars Ignite**

In the velvet sky, secrets lie,
Slumbering stars twinkle on high.
When night descends with a gentle sigh,
Dreams awaken, ready to fly.

Constellations weave through the night,
Stories caught in celestial light.
Each glow ignites a whispered prayer,
In cosmic realms, we wander there.

As moonlight bathes the sleeping ground,
The world holds its breath, silence profound.
With every blink, a tale unfurls,
Through timeless skies, dreams swirl and twirl.

Infinite wonders stretch on and on,
In starlit depths, our fears are gone.
They whisper softly, guiding our way,
In this embrace, eternally stay.

Slumbering stars, ancient and wise,
In their glow, our spirit thrives.
As dawn approaches, we hold the light,
Knowing dreams will reignite tonight.

## **Resurgence in Radiance**

In shadows deep where silence lay,
A spark ignites, igniting day.
Whispers dance on morning's breath,
Life awakens from its death.

Colors rise, reclaiming skies,
With every hue, new hope implies.
The world transforms, a fresh embrace,
Resurgence blooms in every space.

Gentle beams through branches weave,
Nature sighs, begins to cleave.
From the ashes, dreams take flight,
In the glow, we find our light.

Each heartbeat echoes, pulsing strong,
In harmony, we find our song.
Together we will stand and shine,
United souls, your light and mine.

A tapestry, life's grand design,
In every thread, the stars align.
Resurgence bold, with love unchained,
In radiant waves, we are reclaimed.

## Lifting Veil of Night

The stars retreat, a soft goodbye,
As whispers fade in twilight's sigh.
A canvas waits, the dawn to break,
With every hue, our hearts awake.

The moonlight dims, its watch now done,
A promise blooms with rising sun.
Shadows lift as colors bloom,
In golden rays, dispelling gloom.

Birds take flight in joyous cheer,
A melody that draws us near.
Each note a call to rise and shine,
Together stepping through the line.

With courage, we embrace the light,
The dark retreats, banished from sight.
With every step, we find our path,
In morning's glow, we escape wrath.

A new horizon, bright and bold,
In every heart, a story told.
We lift the veil, explore the day,
In unity, we'll find our way.

## The Rebirth of Dawn

The night releases its last hold,
As dreams dissolve, the light unfolds.
A gentle touch, the sun awakes,
With every rise, the earth remakes.

Soft whispers call through fields anew,
The morning's breath, a tender hue.
Life unfurls in endless grace,
The rebirth shines on every face.

With warmth and light, our spirits soar,
In every heart, we yearn for more.
Take a step, feel the embrace,
In dawn's rebirth, we find our place.

Nature sings, a vibrant song,
In joyous chords, we all belong.
The day ignites, a blazing fire,
In each of us, a deep desire.

So let us rise and greet the morn,
With open hearts, we are reborn.
The dawn is ours, embraced with cheer,
In every ray, our dreams are clear.

## **Glimmering Hope**

In darkest woods where shadows dwell,
A flicker stirs, a secret spell.
With every pulse, the heartbeats grow,
A glimmer shines, a hope to sow.

Through bitter winds and silent cries,
We search the stars, we seek the skies.
In distant lands, a light appears,
A beacon bright, dispelling fears.

Each step we take, through thorns and pain,
Together we will rise again.
In unity, our strength will bind,
A force unseen, yet well-defined.

So hold the light, let it ascend,
With every breath, our spirits blend.
In shared resolve, we find our voice,
In glimmering hope, we make our choice.

Let dreams ignite in hearts ablaze,
With every dawn, our spirits raise.
For in this world, so rich and wide,
Hope's glimmer shines; we walk with pride.

## The Resurgence of the Heart

In quiet moments, whispers start,
A faded flame ignites the dark.
Old dreams awaken, rising tall,
Embracing light, they break the fall.

Fragments lost now intertwine,
With hope as guide, we redesign.
Each beat a promise, pure and bright,
To love again, to find our light.

The journey long, yet worth the fate,
With scars like maps, our hearts narrate.
Resilience sings through every scar,
The phoenix rises, ever far.

In every heartbeat, passion sings,
The joy of life, the hope it brings.
Together we bloom, in colors bold,
A tapestry of hearts retold.

From ashes new, we paint the sky,
A resurgence fierce, we dare to try.
United in spirit, we shall stand,
As love's soft whisper guides our hand.

## Shadows Turn to Stories

In twilight's grasp, the shadows blend,
Secrets whispered, journeys end.
Stories linger, etched in time,
Echoes call, a haunting rhyme.

With every darkness, light does shift,
Unraveling tales, a timeless gift.
From silence blooms the voice we seek,
In shadows deep, our spirits speak.

In every corner, tales arise,
Wisdom wrapped in silent cries.
The past unfolds with every breath,
Each memory lives, defying death.

We dance with ghosts, embracing fate,
Their stories weave our soul's estate.
From shadows cast, we seek the sun,
In unity, we are all one.

Light reveals what once was veiled,
With every heartbeat, truth unveiled.
In stories shared, our hearts unite,
The shadows fade, we find the light.

## Glimmers of Truth Emerging

In quiet dawn, the mist will break,
A hint of hope, a chance to wake.
Emerging truths like blossoms bloom,
Dispelling doubt, dispelling gloom.

With every step, the path unfolds,
In whispered tales, the heart beholds.
Glimmers bright, we chase the light,
Compassion lifting us from night.

Through trials faced, the courage grows,
A river flows where wisdom knows.
In truth's embrace, we find release,
An inner calm, a soul at peace.

Each lesson learned, a precious thread,
Woven tightly, where we've tread.
In glimmers bright, we trust the way,
With truth as guide, we greet the day.

From shadows past, we step anew,
Embracing all, both brave and true.
In every heart, a light will shine,
As glimmers rise, we intertwine.

## A Candle in the Abyss

In darkest nights when hope seems lost,
A flicker glows, we bear the cost.
A candle burns with gentle grace,
Illuminating our lonely space.

With every flame, we set the tone,
A beacon bright, we are not alone.
Through shadows deep, it guides our way,
In moments bleak, it holds the sway.

Its warmth embraces every fear,
A steadfast light that draws us near.
With every flicker, dreams ignite,
In courage found, we rise with might.

Against the void, our spirits dance,
In darkness deep, we take our chance.
A candle's glow, a love's embrace,
With every heartbeat, we find our place.

Through trials faced, we hold it high,
A flame of truth that will not die.
In the abyss, we make our stand,
As light persists, we join the band.

**The Canvas of Renewal**

In the dawn's soft embrace we awaken,
With colors of hope brightly shaken.
Nature whispers in tones of rebirth,
Each moment a gift, a treasure of worth.

The skies blaze with a fiery hue,
Telling tales of the past, yet anew.
Blossoms unfold, in dance they play,
Turning the old into vibrant display.

Streams hum a tune, pure and clear,
Carving paths that wander near.
From shadows of doubt, we take our flight,
Guided by the sun's warm light.

In this tapestry woven with grace,
Every heartbeat finds its place.
Let paintbrushes linger, don't swiftly move,
For in stillness, we find our groove.

With each stroke, the spirit ignites,
Boundless dreams soar to new heights.
Together we craft a world of delight,
A canvas of renewal in soft twilight.

## Starlight's Embrace

Under the blanket where dreams reside,
Stars whisper secrets in the night wide.
They twinkle softly, like a muse's sigh,
Inviting our hearts to learn how to fly.

The moon graces gently with silver beams,
Warming our souls with celestial dreams.
Each twinkling light, a wish taken flight,
Guiding weary travelers through dark into light.

In this silence, echoes softly sing,
Of moments like jewels, pure and spring.
With every glance, our spirits convene,
Bound by the threads of the universe's sheen.

Galaxies swirl in a dance so divine,
Time stands still, as our hearts align.
Wrapped in starlight, we find our place,
In the vastness of night, an infinite embrace.

As dawn breaks the spell, we hold these sights,
Memories whispered in the starry nights.
Starlight's embrace lives on in our hearts,
Guiding our journey as each new day starts.

## **The Light Beyond the Veil**

Behind the curtain where shadows reside,
A flicker of truth waits to be spied.
Veils of illusion, they softly entwine,
Yet hope beckons, a pathway divine.

With every whisper, the fog starts to part,
Illuminating the rise of the heart.
A gentle glow, like a candle's soft flame,
Inviting the lost, with courage, to claim.

In the depths of silence, clarity gleams,
Opening windows to echo our dreams.
Through layers unseen, the light weaves its way,
Reminding us all that the dawn holds sway.

With courage ignited, we seek and we find,
The glimmers of magic that life intertwined.
Beyond what is seen, the essence reveals,
A journey of heart where each truth heals.

So draw back that veil, let your spirit soar,
Embrace the light that awaits at the door.
For in every shadow, there lies a tale,
Of strength and wisdom, the light beyond the veil.

# A Flicker in the Gloom

In the depths where the echoes of sorrow dwell,
A flicker remains, a soft-spoken bell.
Amidst the dark, in a world filled with strife,
A whisper of hope stirs the edges of life.

With courage like embers, we fan the soft flame,
Finding our footing, we rise not in shame.
The shadows may linger, yet we draw near,
To the glow of the light that beckons with cheer.

Every heartbeat mirrors the struggle we face,
Yet flickers of joy leave a warm trace.
In moments of quiet, we gather our might,
Like fireflies dancing, we shine in the night.

Let laughter emerge from the depths of despair,
Illuminating paths, unkindness laid bare.
With love as our lantern, our voices unite,
We share in the glow, igniting the night.

So treasure that flicker, let it lead the way,
For even in gloom, a new dawn will play.
Together, we rise from the ashes that loom,
Crafting our future from a flicker in the gloom.

## Rise of the Phoenix

From ashes deep, a flame ignites,
Wings unfurling, taking flight.
Resilience born from trials past,
A symbol of hope, forever vast.

With fiery hues that pierce the dusk,
In the face of doubt, we trust.
The sky awakes, a canvas bold,
Stories of triumph, waiting to be told.

Upward soars, through storm and rage,
A dance of life, a sacred stage.
In every heartbeat, embers glow,
A journey onward, ever so.

With every rise, a deeper fall,
But in rise, we hear the call.
A cycle endless, bright and new,
For every end, a world to view.

So let the flames consume our fears,
In unity, we shed our tears.
The Phoenix thrives, a lesson clear,
In every struggle, love draws near.

## Breaking the Chains of Night

In shadows cast, the silence grows,
A whisper lost, where darkness flows.
Yet from the depths, a spark ignites,
A fragile hope in endless nights.

Beneath the weight, we softly tread,
With dreams that flourish, never dead.
A light emerges, piercing through,
Each heartbeat strong, a promise true.

We rise together, hand in hand,
To brave the storm and take a stand.
With every step, the chains do break,
For every dawn, a chance to wake.

The night may linger, but we persist,
With every shadow, a twist of fate.
Our voices join in chorus bright,
Together strong, we chase the light.

So fear not darkness, for love will lead,
A beacon of hope, a heart that bleeds.
In unity, we break the chains,
For in the light, our power reigns.

## Portrait of Brightness

A canvas spread with colors wide,
Each stroke a tale, a hidden guide.
In vibrant hues, the story flows,
A dance of light, where beauty grows.

The sunbeam kisses the morning dew,
Nature awakes in bursts of hue.
Every petal sings a song,
In this mosaic, we belong.

With laughter shared, the moments gleam,
A tapestry woven, an endless dream.
In each glance, a spark ignites,
A portrait framed in warm delights.

As shadows fade, the brilliance glows,
Through heart and spirit, love bestows.
In every soul, a canvas bright,
Together, we become the light.

Embrace the colors, feel their grace,
In every heartbeat, find your place.
For life's a journey, bright and vast,
A portrait cherished, forever cast.

## Rays Beneath the Shadows

In the quiet hush of fading light,
The shadows dance, an endless flight.
Yet underneath, a warmth resides,
In hidden rays, where hope abides.

Among the dark, a flicker shines,
Guiding lost hearts through tangled vines.
Each ray a promise, soft and true,
Whispers of love breaking through.

The night may cloak the world outside,
But in our hearts, the light won't hide.
In every struggle, we find the way,
For dawn awaits with a brand new day.

With every trial, we grow more bold,
Through stormy skies, our spirits hold.
For even in sorrow, bright paths unfold,
In shadows deep, our stories told.

So rise with courage, face the dark,
Embrace the light, ignite the spark.
In unity, our hearts collide,
For rays of hope will always guide.

## Illuminating the Unknown

In shadows deep, we dare to tread,
Where whispers dwell and dreams are fed.
The night reveals what day obscures,
A world profound, with hidden cures.

With every step, the light unfolds,
Mysteries wrapped in stories told.
We seek the paths that seem forlorn,
As stars above, our souls are born.

In silence vast, the heart aligns,
With echoes soft, the spirit shines.
Embrace the chance, let courage flow,
For in the dark, new wonders grow.

Beneath the veil, a dance begins,
The beauty found in what life spins.
Through labyrinths of thought and fear,
We find the truth that draws us near.

So take a breath, and step anew,
For every night brings dawn's debut.
With visions clear, we rise above,
And shine with warmth, like stars in love.

## Breath of New Beginnings

When morning breaks, a canvas clear,
Fresh hopes arise, and dreams appear.
The dawn ignites, a vibrant glow,
With every heartbeat, life will flow.

From ashes past, we craft the new,
With colors bold, and skies of blue.
Each step we take, a tale unfolds,
With whispered truths and courage bold.

The winds of change, they gently call,
To rise above, to never fall.
In every breath, the chance is found,
To weave our fate from thoughts profound.

As petals bloom, the heart takes flight,
With open arms, we greet the light.
A symphony of joy and grace,
Awaits us all, in time's embrace.

So let us dance on paths anew,
With every smile, a world in view.
For life's a gift, a fleeting song,
With every note, we all belong.

## Ascent to Brilliance

In valleys low, we find our way,
With hopes ignited by the day.
We climb with strength, towards the peak,
Where dreams converge, and souls can speak.

Each step we take, the air grows thin,
With every challenge, we begin.
The view expands, horizons wide,
Awakening the joy inside.

Through storms we rise, through fears we soar,
With courage fierce, we seek for more.
The heart ignites when trials call,
We rise united, never fall.

In heights unknown, our spirits blend,
With every chance, our wills ascend.
Together strong, we shine like rays,
Illuminating countless ways.

So let us forge, with hearts ablaze,
A brighter path through life's fair maze.
For in this quest, we carve our name,
Ascent to brilliance, life's sweet flame.

## Threads of Dawn

In morning's glow, the threads unwind,
We weave the dreams that life designed.
With every stitch, a story born,
As night retreats, we greet the morn.

Each color bright, a memory's thread,
Of laughter shared, of tears once shed.
With hope in hand, we craft anew,
The tapestry of me and you.

The sun will rise, and shadows fade,
With every heartbeat, fears cascade.
We hold the loom of time and space,
Creating beauty, love's embrace.

As dawn unfolds, our hearts align,
In unity, the stars will shine.
With every breath, a chance to grow,
In life's vast quilt, we're not alone.

So take the threads, both dark and light,
And weave your truth with all your might.
For in this dance, we find our way,
Threads of dawn, a brand new day.

## Refracting Pain into Beauty

In shadows deep, a tear may fall,
Yet in its glimmer, truth stands tall.
The heartache blooms like a fragile rose,
Transforming pain where the wild wind blows.

Resilience whispers in the night,
Crafting colors from fading light.
Each scar, a brushstroke on canvas bare,
A testament to battles, beyond despair.

From ashes rise, the phoenix song,
A symphony where sorrow belongs.
In broken pieces, a mosaic made,
Crafting beauty from the serenade.

Such alchemy in the soul's embrace,
Turning hardships into grace.
With every heartbeat, hope ignites,
Refractions dance in glowing lights.

## Heartbeats of Morning

Dawn creeps softly, the world awakes,
A melody of life, a new day makes.
Each heartbeat echoes in the stillness,
Promises held in morning's fullness.

The sun will rise, a golden flame,
Chasing shadows, igniting names.
Birdsong weaves through trees so tall,
Nature's anthem, a joyful call.

Beneath the skies, a tender hue,
Refreshes dreams, births something new.
As petals unfold, kissed by dew,
Daylight dances, painting the view.

With every heartbeat, time flows on,
In every breath, the past is gone.
Tomorrow's promise glimmers bright,
In the heartbeats of morning light.

## **Beyond the Veil of Sorrow**

In silence wrapped, the shadows creep,
A world of whispers where secrets sleep.
Yet through the veil, a light may shine,
Guiding lost souls toward the divine.

Each tear a river, flowing clear,
Carving paths through doubt and fear.
In sorrow's grip, we seek to find,
The echoes of love in hearts entwined.

The night may cloak, but hope still glows,
In every heartbeat, resilience grows.
A tapestry woven from threads of pain,
Beyond the veil, the sun will reign.

So stand we firm, through trials faced,
With courage bold, and dreams embraced.
For after storms, the skies will part,
And heal the wounds within the heart.

## Pathways to Radiance

In every step, a choice we make,
Through winding paths, our spirits quake.
Yet on this journey, light will break,
Transforming shadows for hope's sweet sake.

Each moment lived, a treasure found,
On dusty trails where dreams are bound.
We navigate the twists and turns,
For every loss, a lesson yearns.

The horizon glows with shades of gold,
A beacon bright for the brave and bold.
In joys discovered, new worlds rise,
Pathways leading to endless skies.

Through valleys low and mountains high,
We chase the stars, we wonder why.
For in our hearts, a fire is stoked,
On pathways to radiance, hope invoked.

## The Embers of Change

In the quiet dawn, whispers of light,
Flicker and dance, shattering the night.
Hope ignites slowly, like a spark,
Kindling the dreams that slept in the dark.

With each soft breath, new pathways unfold,
Stories untold, in layers of gold.
Time bends and twists, a canvas so bright,
Painting new futures, igniting the fight.

The embers of change burn fiercely inside,
Guiding our hearts, where shadows abide.
We learn and we grow, through trials and tears,
Transforming our fears into strength through the years.

In the ashes lie seeds of what's yet to be,
Transformation's promise, vibrant and free.
As night turns to morning, we rise once more,
Embracing the change, we're ready to soar.

Each ember whispers of journeys unknown,
Stoking the fires of courage we've grown.
With hearts wide open, we rise and we sing,
To the rhythm of change, life's beautiful fling.

## A Symphony in Colors

In the garden of dreams, colors collide,
Brushstrokes of nature, a vibrant tide.
Petals of laughter, hues of the heart,
Each note a story, a delicate art.

The azure skies weep, and then they smile,
With golden sunbeams that warm for a while.
Saffron sunsets paint the evening air,
A symphony swells, in colors we share.

Emerald whispers of leaves in a dance,
Twirl with the breeze, in a fragrant romance.
From crimson dawns to the indigo night,
Each splash of color, a jubilant sight.

As raindrops fall, the palette expands,
Mingling the shades with the love in our hands.
In every hue, a heartbeat's refrain,
Resonating softly, like sweet gentle rain.

Together we paint, in unison found,
A canvas of hopes, where magic is bound.
A symphony rises, let melodies soar,
In this world of colors, we're always wanting more.

## Rejuvenation of the Soul

In the stillness of dawn, breaths become free,
Nature awakens, inviting you to be.
Gentle whispers of wind, soft to the touch,
Carrying hopes that mean so much.

Beneath ancient trees, roots intertwine,
Cradling stories, both yours and mine.
Each moment unfolds like petals in spring,
Rejuvenation's song, like a bird on the wing.

Savor the silence, let worries decay,
Find solace in stillness, let confusion sway.
With every heartbeat, a rhythm of peace,
In the arms of the universe, feel your release.

Through trials and storms, we learn to prevail,
Rising like phoenixes, our spirits set sail.
The essence of life pulses deep within,
Guiding our journey, where hope will begin.

Embrace the renewal, let shadows dissolve,
In the light of forgiveness, our souls will evolve.
Together we wander, with hearts that are whole,
Celebrating the beauty of life, the soul.

As day turns to night, we honor the shift,
In every new dawn lies a powerful gift.
Rejuvenate deeply, let spirits entwine,
For each day is precious, a new chance to shine.

## The Other Side of Twilight

In twilight's embrace, the world holds its breath,
A dance of the shadows, a whisper of death.
The stars gently twinkle in indigo skies,
As dreams weave their magic in shimmering ties.

A canvas of silence, the colors cascade,
Moments of wonder, where fears start to fade.
The horizon beckons, with secrets untold,
Inviting us softly, to venture and hold.

In the twilight's grip, we find clarity's flame,
Past echoes of sorrow, lost in a name.
Each flicker of light is a guide for the lost,
Illuminating paths, whatever the cost.

As day yields to night, we reflect and we dream,
Embracing the stillness, the gentle esteem.
The whispers of twilight cradle our fears,
Turning them sacred, drying our tears.

Through dusk we are led, to the night's quiet song,
With hope as our lantern, we cannot go wrong.
In every heartbeat, the magic survives,
For on the other side, true beauty derives.

So pause in the twilight, and listen with care,
The pulse of the universe, magic to share.
With hearts open wide, let the stars be our guide,
On the other side of twilight, love will abide.

## Shadows Unbound

In whispers deep, the shadows play,
They dance in silence, night and day.
They stretch and leap, and twist in grace,
Unbound they roam, each hidden space.

Across the moonlit, misty ground,
In every corner, secrets found.
They weave a tale of lost refrain,
In darkness' clutch, they hold their reign.

The fleeting light, they seek to shun,
In twilight's grasp, their games begun.
Each flicker dims, as shadows creep,
Where fears awaken, dreams may weep.

A playful chase, a fleeting spark,
In shadow's arms, we leave our mark.
With every step, the stories blend,
In shadows' sway, they never end.

So wander forth, through night's embrace,
In shadowed realms, find your own space.
For in the dark, all fears unbound,
In mystery's heart, joy can be found.

## Embrace of Radiance

Beneath the sun's soft golden rays,
Life thrums in vibrant, joyful plays.
Each petal opens, colors bright,
In nature's arms, an endless light.

The whispers of the morning dew,
Awake the dreams of every hue.
A tapestry of life unfolds,
In radiant warmth, our hearts are bold.

With every heartbeat, warmth we bring,
In harmony, let our voices sing.
The whispers flow, like rivers wide,
In radiance, we will abide.

As shadows fall, they fade away,
In golden moments, we will stay.
Embraced by light, our souls will soar,
A bond unbreakable, evermore.

So let us dance within this glow,
For love ignites what we both know.
In every heartbeat, spark resides,
In the embrace, our spirit guides.

**The Awakening Glow**

As dawn awakens, light does spread,
A gentle touch upon the bed.
The world ignites, in colors bright,
Awakening dreams, banishing night.

Each shadow fades, as warmth unfolds,
Revealing whispers, tales retold.
New beginnings breathe anew,
In the awakening, joy breaks through.

The heartbeat of the morning air,
Carries with it, hope and care.
With every sunbeam, spirits rise,
Chasing clouds in endless skies.

Let petals open, hearts embrace,
In the gentle light, find your place.
For every dawn is life's rebirth,
A promise born from Mother Earth.

So stand and greet the rising sun,
In every moment, life's begun.
With open hearts, let's dance and flow,
Together, lost in the awakening glow.

## Journey Through the Abyss

In shadows thick, the whispers call,
A journey waits through darkness' hall.
With every step, the unknown calls,
In silent depths, our courage sprawls.

The echoes echo, tales of fate,
In twilight's grip, we contemplate.
Through veils of night, a path unclear,
Yet deeper truths draw ever near.

With lanterns dimmed, we seek the light,
Through twisted paths of endless night.
Each heartbeat's pounding, steady, true,
In darkness' grasp, our souls renew.

The abyss may whisper tales of dread,
But through the shadows, hope is fed.
With every fall, we learn to rise,
In journey's depths, our strength lies.

So fear not, wanderer, take your stride,
In darkness, dreams may still abide.
Through every challenge, we shall grow,
In the abyss, our spirits glow.

**Singularity of Dawn**

A whisper of light spills wide,
Awakening dreams once tucked inside.
The horizon blushes with soft hues,
As night yields to the day's bright fuse.

Birdsong breaks the morning's chill,
Nature breathes, the world stands still.
Dewdrops shimmer on blades of grass,
Moments of peace in morning's class.

The sky unfurls a canvas clear,
Colorful reminders that spring is near.
Each ray dances on sleepy land,
A gentle touch, a guiding hand.

In this singularity we find,
A promise of hope, a dream aligned.
The past dissolves, new paths unfold,
With every dawn, a story told.

So let us cherish this new start,
Embrace the day, open our heart.
For in the dawn's warm embrace,
Lies the beauty of time and space.

## The Dance of Dusk and Dawn

In twilight's glow, colors entwine,
A waltz of shadows, soft and fine.
Day bows to night, a graceful blend,
As whispers of light and dark contend.

Stars awaken, the moon takes flight,
A gentle nod to fading light.
The horizon sighs, its canvas draped,
With shades of eve, softly shaped.

Dawn peeks in, a timid flame,
Igniting moments, never the same.
The two embrace, then drift apart,
A fleeting kiss, a tender heart.

In the dance of dusk and dawn,
New stories rise and old are drawn.
With every step, the cycle turns,
In life's great theatre, the passion burns.

So watch the sky, let your spirit soar,
As day and night forever explore.
Their dance a rhythm, a timeless play,
In the bond of dusk and dawn, we stay.

## Radiant Within

Beneath the surface, light does dwell,
In shadows deep, where secrets tell.
A gentle spark, a flicker of grace,
Reminds us of our inner space.

Amidst the chaos, find the calm,
A refuge whispered, a soothing balm.
With each heartbeat, the glow expands,
A warmth that lingers, a love that stands.

The world may dim, but we will shine,
Our souls a beacon, a sacred sign.
In every breath, the light reveals,
The truth in us that softly heals.

So let your spirit dance and sway,
Embrace the whispers, come what may.
For in the stillness, we discover,
The radiant light we all can uncover.

Hold fast to hope, in moments bleak,
For within you lies the strength you seek.
A luminous heart, a guide for all,
In love's embrace, we will not fall.

## When Night Meets Day

In the quiet, shadows blend,
Night stretches out, day will wend.
A symphony of colors starts,
As twilight plays its subtle parts.

Stars twinkle, bidding goodbye,
As warm hues paint the evening sky.
The moon whispers in silver tones,
Glimmers dance on abandoned stones.

When night meets day, dreams ignite,
Hope awakens in soft twilight.
A moment captured, fleeting, clear,
Where silence filled with whispers near.

As dawn creeps in, it takes its bow,
Gifting the world a golden vow.
Together they breathe, a blend divine,
In the canvas of time, eternally entwined.

So witness this magic, pure and bright,
When darkness and daylight unite.
For in their embrace, we find our way,
A journey begins when night meets day.

Milton Keynes UK
Ingram Content Group UK Ltd.
UKHW022119251124
451529UK00012B/610